First Published in 2009 by

OM BOOKS INTERNATIONAL

4379/4B Prakash House
Ansari Road, Darya Ganj
New Delhi 110002
India

Tel: +91-11-23263363
Fax: +91-11-23278091

Email: sales@ombooks.com
www.ombooks.com

ISBN 978-81-87108-48-1

Printed in Malaysia by Tien Wah Press

THE BADA IMAMBARA Built by the erstwhile Nawab of Lucknow in 1784 as a charitable project, the Islamic building is said to be the world's largest arched room without any pillars.

India

Over the Ages

The roots of the Indian culture can be traced back to the Indus Valley civilisation in 2500 BC. Excavations at the main cities of Mohenjodaro and Harappa show evidence of an advanced urban culture with brick buildings, paved roads, drainage and sanitation. These markers of development – a written script, a system of trade and the practice of weaving and metallurgy – shaped the foundation of the Indian civilisation.

The Indus Valley civilisation was replaced by the Vedic period, ushered by the Aryans who migrated from central Asia between 1500 to 1300 BC. The Vedic culture introduced a hierarchical society, divided by occupation, and a religion centred on nature worship, prayers and sacrifices, which became the basis of the caste system and Hinduism. During the Vedic Age, oral traditions of the Aryans were compiled into the Vedas and the Upanishads – the classic texts on Hindu culture, philosophy and religion.

THE EMERGENCE OF NEW RELIGIONS AND EMPIRES

The 6th century BC was a turning point in the Indian history as it saw the birth of new faiths – Buddhism and Jainism – followed by the coming of Christians, Jews and Zoroastrians into India. Politically, the period from 321 BC to 1278 AD witnessed the rise of the Mauryan empire (321–104 BC) and the Gupta empire (319–467 AD) in North India and the Pallava and Chola dynasties (600–1278 AD) in South India. Collectively, it was marked by advances in all fields – from astronomy, mathematics and medicine, to literature and arts – that gradually spread to other contemporary civilisations and influenced their cultures.

FOREIGN INFLUENCES

From the 10th century AD, a succession of Turkish invaders plundered India and eventually defeated the ruling Rajputs to establish the Delhi Sultanate in 1192 AD. Henceforth, Islam became a dominant socio-political force in North India that continued with the Mughal conquest of India in 1526 AD.

The Mughals, who hailed from Samarkand in central Asia, ruled India for over 300 years (1526–1858 AD). The Great Mughal Emperors – Babur, Humayun, Akbar, Jehangir, Shah Jehan and Aurangzeb – were responsible for unifying India into a consolidated empire and inspiring a cultural renaissance unparalleled in the history of this country. The impact of this can still be seen in Indian literature, arts, crafts, architecture and cuisine.

FROM BRITISH RULE TO INDEPENDENCE

Vasco da Gama awakened the European interest in India by discovering a new route in 1498. The decline of the Mughal Empire created a power vacuum that the British were quick to exploit. The British East India Company, established in 1600, amassed a fortune in trade which they used to fund the military campaigns of local kings. By conquering or annexing large territories from Indian rulers, the East India Company became a ruling force in India by the 18th century. After the Revolt of 1857, their acquisitions were transferred to the Crown and became a part of the British Empire.

The British built great cities and spread the benefits of modernisation throughout their empire. But they could not suppress the people's desire for self government, which reached a peak in the 1940s under the leadership of Mahatma Gandhi. Gandhi launched a nation-wide non-violent, mass movement that unified the entire country in a freedom struggle, culminating in the declaration of India's Independence on 15 August 1947. In 1950, India became a Republic with Jawaharlal Nehru and Rajendra Prasad as the first Prime Minister and President, respectively, of the Independent India.

Heritage Sights 🐦

India has 27 UNESCO World Heritage Sites, listed among the 780 wonders of the world. Of these, 22 are unique cultural destinations and 5 are among the world's nature reserves. No other country in the world offers such a vast variety of World Heritage Sites that include world famous monuments, historic cities and forts, religious sites, wildlife parks and sanctuaries, and even a historic mountain railway. For the cultural traveller, India offers an opportunity to study historical monuments that represent pinnacles of artistic and architectural achievements of Indian civilisation. It's a journey of discovery that covers a breathtaking span of history from the earliest human settlements in pre-historic caves to landmarks of modern times. Along the way are rewarding glimpses of great empires, forgotten cities and cultures that speak eloquently of the wonder that was India. Agra and Delhi, as former Mughal capitals, preserve a wealth of monuments, many of which are UNESCO World Heritage Sites, the most popular being the Taj Mahal.

Top: The Taj Mahal is characterised by its perfect proportions and symmetry. Set on a marble terrace, it is surrounded by four graceful minarets, and flanked by a mosque on the west and a similar structure to the east to create a symmetrical setting. The garden is also divided into four quarters by water channels and marble pools, designed to reflect its perfection.

THE TAJ MAHAL

The Taj Mahal is the world's most famous monument. India's poet-laureate Rabindranath Tagore described it as "a teardrop on the face of eternity". This white marble tomb in Agra, built by the Mughal Emperor Shah Jehan in 1650 to commemorate his wife Mumtaz Mahal, represents the finest expression of Mughal art and architecture.

It took a work force of 20,000, including many skilled Persian and Indian craftsmen, and nearly 22 years to build the monument. The main design, considered to be the most perfect expression of India-Islamic architecture, is credited to Ustad Ahmed Lahauri. It is a combination of elements from Persian, Turkish, Indian and Islamic architectural styles.

The tomb's setting is designed to symbolise the Muslim ideal of a garden paradise. The Taj replicates this vision in a classic Mughal garden, landscaped with water bodies set against the backdrop of the Yamuna river, representing the flowing streams of paradise. Attracting two to four million visitors annually, the Taj features in all listings of the seven wonders of the world.

THE GREAT MAUSOLEUMS

QUTUB MINAR

The Qutub Minar is Delhi's landmark – a 72.5 m tower built in 1199 AD by Qutubuddin Aibak, the first Muslim Sultan of Delhi, to commemorate his conquest of North India. Qutubuddin built the first level of this five-storey tower that was completed by his successor, Illtutmish. This dynasty, known as the Slave Dynasty, was in such a hurry to build Muslim monuments that it razed Hindu and Jain temples and plundered material from the rubble. The complex contains some of the earliest Muslim monuments in India, including Delhi's first mosque, the tomb of Illtutmish and the Alai Darwaza, a gateway built by Allauddin Khilji. This site also includes the ruins of the Hindu citadel of Lal Kot, one of the seven cities of Delhi.

Below Left to Right: Latticed windows around Imam Zamin's tomb; Columns with Hindu carvings in the mosque at Qutub Minar.

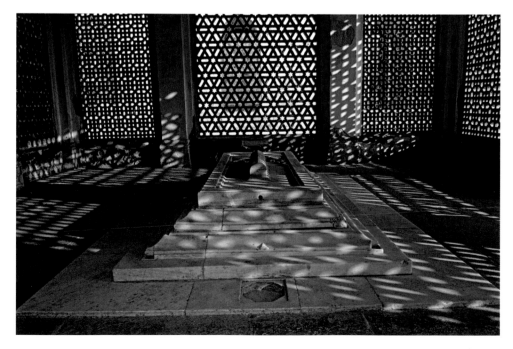

FATEHPUR SIKRI

The city of Fatehpur Sikri, 40 km from Agra, is significant for its architectural legacy. It served as Emperor Akbar's capital for 14 years, till it was abandoned suddenly. In its heyday, it was one of India's first planned cities, remarkable for a layout that followed the topography of the site rather than conventional practices of alignment. The result was an innovative arrangement of buildings around open courtyards and squares that created dramatic spatial effects. The buildings are also an interesting amalgam of Hindu and Muslim architecture, representing the fusion of cultures introduced in Akbar's reign. As an experiment in town planning and design, it continues to inspire modern architects even today.

HUMAYUN'S TOMB

Located in New Delhi, the tomb of Humayun, the second Mughal Emperor, was built in 1570. It is the first example of a Mughal mausoleum that served as a model for the Taj Mahal. Commissioned by Humayun's widow, Haji Begum, this red sandstone edifice, decorated with bands of marble, presents an impression of grandeur. Set in the centre of a traditional Mughal garden, the mausoleum is dominated by a two-storey, octagonal hall punctuated by large arched recesses on all sides and topped by a white marble dome. Though the tomb's architect was Persian, the craftsmen were Indian. This accounts for Hindu features like latticed screens and domed cupolas that were first introduced here and became a prominent feature of the Mughal style.

QUTUB MINAR
The five-storey tower has
exquisite stalactite designs and
bands of calligraphic inscriptions
on its exterior.

ARTISTIC AND ARCHITECTURAL SPLENDOURS

ELEPHANTA CAVES, MUMBAI

Situated on an island in the middle of Mumbai harbour is a remarkable cave temple, sheltering masterpieces of Indian sculpture dating back to the 6th century AD. Originally called Gharapuri or the Fort City, this island was ceded to the Portuguese, who renamed it Elephanta after a large statue of an elephant that stood here. The caves, excavated from a rocky cliff, are adorned with monolithic sculptures and bas reliefs depicting the many forms of the Hindu god Shiva. The most impressive is a three-headed image of Shiva as the Preserver, Creator and Destroyer of the Universe and a sculpture celebrating the marriage of Shiva and his consort Parvati.

Left: The sculptures of Buddha date back to the 4th century and are characterised by graceful forms and expressions that exude a feeling of serenity and calm.

AJANTA CAVES, AURANGABAD

An accidental discovery by a British captain on a hunting expedition in 1619 revealed a treasure house of Buddhist art and architecture in the Sahyadri hills near Aurangabad. This complex of 30 caves arranged around a horseshoe ridge was a monastic retreat for Buddhist monks from 200 BC to 650 AD. The caves include two types of Buddhist architecture – the Chaityas (prayer halls) and the Viharas (monasteries) – that were painstakingly excavated from the volcanic rock face over hundreds of years. The frescoes and sculptures displayed here were the source for Buddhist iconography in Southeast Asia and the Far East.

Left: The Kailash temple, a World Heritage monument, is the focal point of Ellora and one of the architectural wonders of the world. Built by Krishna I of the Rashtrakuta dynasty in the 8th century AD, it is the largest monolithic structure in the world. Designed to symbolise Mount Kailash (the mythic abode of Shiva in the Himalayas), the temple rises from an open courtyard to a height of 81 m, spanning 41 m across. The most amazing fact is that it was excavated by masons who chiselled about 85,000 cu m of solid rock by hand. This three-storey structure was built from the top down, testifying to the architectural and mathematical skills of its builders. As each level was excavated, it was decorated by sculptors, so scaffolding was not necessary. This was a pilgrimage site for Hindus and used for worship till the 19th century.

ELLORA CAVES, AURANGABAD

Ellora, located 26 km north of Aurangabad, is known for its spectacular rock-cut architecture – of which the finest example is the Kailash Temple – and monumental caves. The 34 caves, constructed between the 5th and 10th century AD, shelter the sanctuaries of three faiths – Buddhist, Hindu and Jain. The Buddhist caves, decorated with sculpted images of Buddha and other divinities from the Buddhist epics, were retreats for monks. The Hindu caves were designed for worship and vibrate with images of gods and goddesses, especially Shiva. Jain cave temples are adorned with images of Mahavir, the founder of Jainism. These caves are embellished with intricate sculpted decorations and wall paintings, of which only fragments remain now.

AJANTA FRESCOES, depicting scenes from the life of Buddha, amaze visitors with their lifelike realism, vivid colours and varied compositions. These tempura paintings executed in exquisite detail reflect the life and culture of the age, and still glow with colours made from minerals and natural dyes. The paintings are arranged like a long frieze and themes are linked from frame to frame.

CENTRES OF DEVOTION

THE TEMPLES OF KHAJURAHO

The temples of Khajuraho in Madhya Pradesh are called a testament to love because their erotic sculptures are based on the *Kama Sutra*, the ancient text on the art of love. These sexual poses were part of the scenes displayed on the façade that was intended to depict a celebration of all aspects of life. Originally there were 85 temples built between the 10th and 11th century AD, of which only 22 have survived. Divided into three groups of Hindu and Jain shrines, they testify to the skill of Indian craftsmanship, as well as the wealth of the Chandela kings who commissioned them. Today, the world comes to Khajuraho to see its art as well as classical dance performances at the annual Dance Festival held here. The temples of Khajuraho are fine examples of Indian temple architecture that followed a traditional layout. They were usually built on a raised platform with an entrance porch and a *mandap* (central hall), leading to the inner sanctum where the deity was installed. A towering turreted roof was topped by a central spire. In Khajuraho, the larger temples have corridors for ritual circulation of the temple and some include outer shrines.

Top: Kandariya Mahadev Temple, Khajuraho.

Right: Carved gateway to the Great Stupa at Sanchi.

THE BUDDHIST STUPAS, SANCHI

Sanchi is a Buddhist site marked by the Great Stupa, the largest Buddhist monument in the country. The stupas at Sanchi – with their elaborate carved gateways and statues – offer a record of the development in Buddhist architecture and sculpture over 1,300 years. Unlike other Buddhist sites, Sanchi was not associated with the life of Buddha but came into prominence in the 3rd century BC when the Great Mauryan Emperor Ashoka erected a brick stupa here to commemorate Buddha's enlightenment. This became a pilgrimage site, sprawling with monasteries, prayer halls and stupas, that flourished till the decline of Buddhism in India. Sanchi's monuments were forgotten till General Taylor rediscovered them in 1818.

THE SUN TEMPLE, KONARK

Located near the village of Konark in Orissa is a stone temple dedicated to Surya, the sun god. In the 13th century, when it was built by King Narsimha I, this was a towering edifice on the eastern seaboard with a 70-m spire. For centuries it was a familiar landmark, known to European mariners as the "Black Pagoda". Legend has it that this temple had powerful magnets embedded in its spire that is said to have magically suspended a throne below it in mid-air. For over 300 years it was damaged by Muslim zeal, eroded by the sea and buried under the sand as the sea receded. It was only in the 20th century that efforts were made to restore the ruins of this architectural wonder.

Famous for its intricate design and architectural details, the Sun Temple belongs to the Kalinga School of Indian Temples with typical curvilinear towers mounted by cupolas. The intricate sculptural carvings enhance its magnificence, making it a popular destination among tourists and pilgrims.

Right: The statue of Surya, the sun god, at the Konark temple.

Below: The base of the Konark temple was designed in the form of a giant chariot pulled by horses, depicting the passage of the sun god across the sky. The 12-wheeled chariot, drawn by seven horses, symbolised a calendar divided into hours, weeks and months. Though the spire has fallen and the main temple is crumbling, the base with its enormous carved wheels is still an impressive sight.

THE SHORE TEMPLE, MAMALLAPURAM

Against a dramatic backdrop of the sea and sky is the shore temple of Mamallapuram (formerly Mahabalipuram) in Tamil Nadu. This region was ruled by the Pallava kings from the 6th to the 9th century AD. Now a UNESCO World Heritage site, it is famed for its temples and sculptures that represent the zenith of the Pallava art and architecture. In the 7th century AD, King Rajasimhavarman built a series of temples here that served as models for the South Indian temple architecture. Only one temple remains of the many that have been swept away by the sea. This solitary temple is a landmark in many ways. Unlike Indian temples that have a single deity, this is dedicated to two gods, Vishnu and Shiva. Instead of being carved from solid rock, this was the first temple to be constructed from blocks of stone. It was oriented to the east so that it could be lit by the rising sun at dawn. At night, it was illuminated and moats of water around the temple created the illusion of a floating shrine. This site includes rock-cut caves and shrines, sculptures and carved raths (chariots). The most famous is Arjuna's Penance or The Descent of the Ganga – the world's largest bas relief carved on the face of two boulders.

Left: The raths at Mamallapuram are rock-cut temples with a domed roof, designed to resemble wooden chariots. These temples were the precursors of rock-cut architecture seen at Ajanta and Ellora. Like the Kailash temple, they were carved from the spire downwards. Of the eight raths, the largest is the Dharmaraja Rath, which has a square hall topped by a vaulted roof.

THE LOST WORLD OF HAMPI

History haunts your footsteps in Hampi. It was once called Vijaynagar (City of Victory), founded on the banks of the Tungabhadra river near the present-day village of Hampi in Karnataka. Vijaynagar (popularly known as Hampi) was the capital of a vast South Indian empire, ruled by a dynasty of Hindu kings from the 14th to the 17th century AD. Planned on surprisingly modern lines, the city had an urban and religious centre and ample civic amenities – roads, water supply and riverside quays for trade and transport. The city's wealthy court and trading centres were visited by ambassadors, travellers and merchants from Goa to Italy. According to some accounts, it rivalled Rome in size and grandeur. A defeat against the Muslims in 1565 left the capital in ruins. The Vijaynagar kings shifted to Andhra Pradesh, from where they ruled a shrinking kingdom till the 17th century. In the 20th century, conservation efforts by UNESCO and the local government attempted to preserve its monuments despite the pressure of economic development following the building of the Tungabhadra Dam.

Top: Mahanavmi Dibba, the eight-tiered platform at Hampi, was probably used for the king's appearance during state functions and festivals.

Left: The 16th-century Vitthala temple, dedicated to Lord Krishna, is the most artistic of the temple complex at Hampi, though it is no longer used for worship. It is adorned with beautiful carved pillars and a unique Garuda shrine in the shape of a chariot. The temple complex has a collection of temples built in the classic Dravidian style, some of which are still in use.

Right: The stone chariot at Vitthala Temple has revolving wheels, each shaped like a lotus.

Royal ⁓ Retreats

The age of royalty comes alive in India's legendary forts and palaces. Perched on lofty cliffs or hilltops, these forts, built by a succession of rulers across India, provided necessary defence against local enemies or foreign invaders. Every fort enclosed a royal citadel with palaces, apartments and pavilions for dining or entertainment. The focal point was the Durbar Hall, the seat of governance, where kings held court. The luxury and splendour of these courts were symbols of a ruler's wealth and power. Today these palaces and forts offer glimpses of a royal lifestyle and many of them have been converted into heritage hotels.

MUGHAL CITADELS

The Mughals were avid builders who left behind a legacy of splendid monuments designed in the Indo-Islamic architectural style – a blend of Persian and Hindu elements that reflected the synthesis of cultures during their reign. The most visible symbols of Mughal power were the forts they built in Agra and Delhi.

THE AGRA FORT, built by Akbar in 1565, is a UNESCO World Heritage Site and was awarded the Aga Khan Award for Architecture in 1995. The fort (facing page), added by three Mughal emperors, contains a complex of palaces, gardens and mosques.

RED FORT, DELHI

When Shah Jehan moved his capital to Delhi in 1571, he built a red sandstone fort, the focal point of the new city of Shahjehanabad. Popularly called *Lal Quila* or Red Fort, it surpassed the courts of Europe in magnificence.

Left: The Peacock throne stands under a marble canopy in the Diwan-i-Am (Hall of Public Audience).

Below: The Indian tricolour flies on top of the Red Fort in Delhi.

ROMANTIC RAJPUT FORTS

AMBER FORT

The citadel of Amber, outside Jaipur, is one of the classic hill forts of Rajasthan. Constructed by Maharaja Man Singh in 1592 on the remains of an old 11th century fort, it overlooks a lake and offers superb views of the surrounding hills. It served as a capital for the Kacchwwa Rajputs till they shifted to the city of Jaipur in 1727. The palace interiors, decorated with frescoes and inlaid mirrors, and formal Mughal gardens conjure romantic images of a royal life.

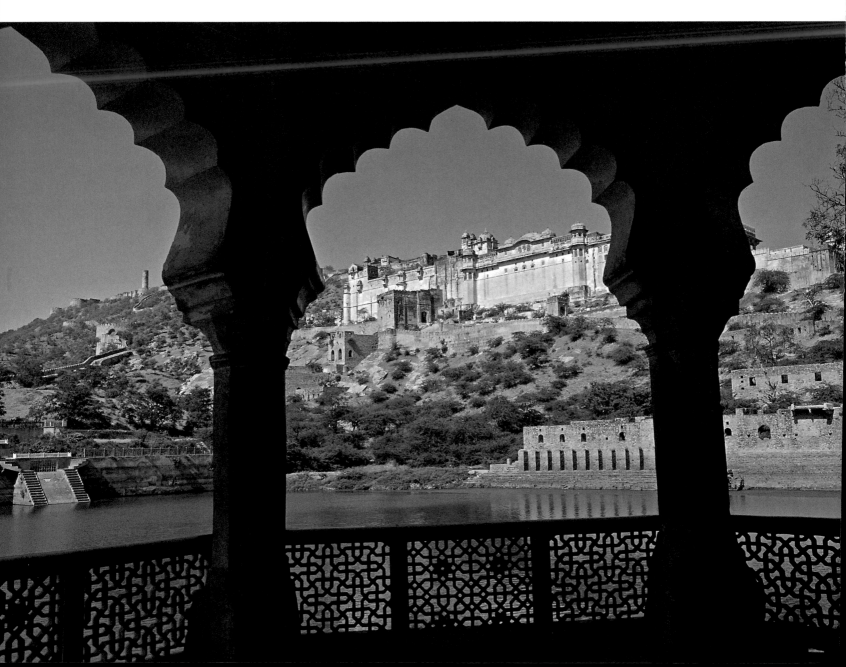

MEHRANGARH FORT

Built by Rao Jodha in 1459, this was a stronghold of the Rathore Rajputs of Jodhpur. In an age of warring kingdoms, Mehrangarh's location on a sheer 91-m cliff was designed to resist invasion. In its 300-year history, this rugged fort, defended by the blood and sacrifice of the Rajputs, never fell into enemy hands.

BASTIONS OF POWER

GOLCONDA FORT

Outside Hyderabad, the granite fort of Golconda (below) was built by the Qutub Shahi dynasty over 62 years. Defended by a 10-km wall, eight gates and bastions mounted by cannons, it was an impressive citadel till its capture by the Mughals. It still impresses visitors with its defences, acoustic effects and interiors cooled by water channels and ventilation ducts.

GWALIOR FORT

Guarding the gateway to central India, Gwalior Fort was considered the most impregnable fortress in India. Its strategic location made it a target of conquest by many, notably Babur, the first Mughal ruler. Spread over 3 km, the fort contains three temples, six palaces, a museum, many dungeons and a pond, which is believed to have cured its founder of leprosy! The palaces, once decorated with colourful tiles, murals and latticed screens, were described by Babur as "the pearl in the necklace of palaces of the Hind".

PLEASURE PALACES

An ancient lineage of kings, courtly traditions and wealth created some of the most beautiful palaces in the princely kingdoms of India. Maharajas rivalled with each other to build pleasure palaces that were the last word in luxury. No expense was spared to create dazzling interiors suitable for royalty. Gold and silver ornamentation, murals and mosaic art, marble floors and screens were the predominant features of the palace decor. Persian carpets, rich furnishings, chandeliers and crystal furniture completed these resplendent settings for royal living.

UMAID BHAWAN, JODHPUR

The Umaid Bhawan Palace in Jodhpur is the world's largest royal residence, set in vast landscaped gardens on the crest of a hill in Jodhpur. Built by Maharaja Umaid Singh in 1943 as a famine relief project, it was constructed over 15 years. Designed by H.V. Lanchester, this is a splendid example of modern palaces created in a blend of Indian and Western styles in the 20th century.

The Umaid Bhawan Palace is still occupied by the royal family though the major portion is now a luxury hotel. Its art deco interiors were designed by Stephan Norblin, an émigré Polish artist, who also executed the magnificent murals in the state rooms and royal suites.

LAKE PALACE, UDAIPUR

Shimmering like a mirage in the waters of Lake Pichola is the white marbled Lake Palace of Udaipur. Designed as a summer retreat for the Maharanas of Udaipur, this palace is one of the most romantic luxury hotels in the world. The royal suites at the Lake Palace, decorated with antiques and mural paintings, offer scenic views of the lake and surrounding hills . . . the perfect setting for an idyllic holiday or a romantic honeymoon.

THE CITY PALACE, JAIPUR

Located in the centre of Jaipur is the City Palace, the residence of the former Maharajas of Jaipur. Built by Maharaja Jai Singh in the early 18th century, it was expanded by his successors to include a complex of royal apartments and public buildings designed in Mughal and Rajput architectural styles. Though the palace is now open to visitors, a part is still occupied by the royal family.

The City Palace Museum has a rare collection of royal finery and artefacts that displays the wealth of Jaipur's maharajas and their patronage of arts and crafts. Two silver urns, acclaimed to be the world's largest silver vessels, are showcased here. These were made to carry the holy water of the Ganga for Sawai Madho Singh II to drink on his trip to England in 1901.

JAI VILAS PALACE, GWALIOR

The grandiose structure of the Jai Vilas Palace in Gwalior was inspired by the palaces of England and Europe. It was built by Maharaja Jayaji Rao Scindia to impress the Prince of Wales (Edward VII) on his visit to India in 1875. Furnished on a grand scale, the palace has a large collection of antiques – French furniture, Persian rugs, Mughal paintings and a silver toy train that conveyed brandy and cigars along the length of a banquet table for 100 guests.

The Assembly Hall of the Jai Vilas Palace houses the world's largest crystal chandeliers, weighing over 3 tonnes. It is said that eight elephants were used to test the strength of the roof before installing the two giant chandeliers.

MYSORE PALACE, KARNATAKA

Mysore Palace may not be as large as the palaces of the north but it is undoubtedly one of the most ornate. This was the home of the Wodeyar kings who ruled the former kingdom of Mysore, near Bangalore. Designed by an English architect, Henry Irwin, it combines elements of South Indian temple decoration within an Indo-Saracenic structure. The Diwan-i- Am (Hall of Public Audience) in Mysore Palace resembles a fairy tale setting with its spectacular gilded columns and ornate ceiling inlaid with gems and fresco paintings. The Maharaja's solid gold throne is displayed here during ceremonial occasions.

Colours of the Desert 〜

The Thar Desert is part of the Great Indian Desert, covering an area of 208,000 sq km across northwest India. The major portion lies in the western region of Rajasthan, known as Marusthali or the Land of Death. According to legend, the Thar was once fertile, watered by rivers that have long since disappeared, leaving fossilised remains of animals and trees as evidence of its pre-historic past. This was the last refuge of the Rajputs, who migrated here following the Muslim invasion of North India in the 12th century AD. The Rajputs established wealthy kingdoms in the citadels of Jaisalmer, Jodhpur and Bikaner. Within their mighty forts, defended by blood and sacrifice, they built magnificent palaces, temples and mansions that fostered patronage of arts and crafts. The struggle to survive has given these people resilience, helping them to colour their barren environment with multicoloured costumes and vibrant celebrations of music and dance.

JAISALMER FORT, a World Heritage Site, houses a collection of exquisite sandstone palaces and mansions, shimmering like a mirage in the heart of the menacing Thar Desert. This architectural wonder showcases amazing craftsmanship, with the palace interiors, adorned with frescoes, mirrors and gilt, displaying the Rajput love for ornamentation.

CATTLE FAIRS combine business with pleasure, featuring stalls for shopping, music and dance performances, camel races and acrobatic shows.

CULTURE

The desert is home to many traditions of folk music and dance that are distinctive to individual castes and communities. These include the Teerah Taali performed by women, balancing a succession of pots on their heads to the sound of cymbals; the Sapera Dance of the snake charmers; Kacchi Godi, where men in elaborate dresses ride on dummy horses and dance to the beats of drums and fifes; and the Ghoomer, a swirling community dance for women, performed on auspicious occasions.

EPIC HISTORY AND FOLK LEGENDS are brought to life by the haunting melodies of the Bhopas, Charans and Manganiyars, the hereditary clans of balladeers, bards and musicians.

PEOPLE Red, orange, hot pink and green are the colours of the desert, seen in the swirling skirts and vibrant veils of the women and the turbans of the men. On the outskirts of Jodhpur live the Bishnois, a clan of traditional environmentalists who are the followers of Jambeshwar, a 15th century sage. They are vegetarians who protect trees and wildlife, especially the blackbuck that roams freely around their hamlets.

Paradises by the Sea

The Indian peninsula, flanked by the waters of the Arabian Sea, the Bay of Bengal and the Indian Ocean, offers the widest variety of beach resorts along its 5,700 km coastline. Stretching from the states of Gujarat and Goa on the west to Orissa in the east, and Kerala and Pondicherry in the south, these destinations encompass a vast range of landscapes – from tropical beaches, scenic lagoons and waterways to sybaritic coral islands and reefs off the mainland.

Since ancient times, India's seaports have been a stopover on the seafaring routes from Europe to the Orient. A succession of traders – Arabs, Chinese, Dutch, Portuguese and English – have left their mark on the architecture, culture and cuisine of the coast, giving many of India's beach resorts a unique ambience and flavour. So, besides the pleasures of sun, sand and surf, beach lovers can discover a heady mix of distinctive cultures and cuisines, along with the rejuvenating benefits of international spas, ayurvedic health resorts and a choice of leisure and water sports.

KERALA Also known as the "God's own country", Kerala is famous for its beaches and extensive backwaters. Kovalam, Cherai and Varkala are the popular beaches, all of which have resorts with ayurvedic parlours, and yoga and meditation centres.

Top: The backwaters of Kerala. The best way to explore Kerala's verdant landscape is by taking a houseboat cruise on its backwaters, offering a taste of Kerala's cuisine and village life.

Below: The beach resorts in Kerala combine the pleasures of a beach holiday with the age-old ayurvedic health and beauty treatments in its spas.

Left: Sculpture of Shiva at Vagator Beach, Goa.

GOA As an international beach resort, Goa has it all. Its idyllic beaches, dotted with world-class tourist resorts, are known for their natural beauty, lively nightlife and water sports. A laid-back lifestyle, superb cuisine, historic churches and heritage homes – a legacy of its past as a former Portuguese colony – offer all the elements of a perfect beach holiday.

ANDAMAN AND NICOBAR ISLANDS

Top: Located in the middle of the Bay of Bengal, Andaman and Nicobar is India's version of Eden. Its dense forests preserve many species of wildlife, while the surrounding sea is known for unique species of marine life.

LAKSHWADEEP, an archipelago of 36 coral islands in the Arabian Sea, is a scuba diver's paradise. The resorts on Bangaram and Kadamat island provide a wilderness experience with deep sea explorations.

DIU, a tiny island off the coast of Gujarat, was once a Portuguese enclave. It offers the attractions of a tranquil beach holiday.

Left: The fort at Diu commands a magnificent view of the sea and its surrounding areas.

PURI

The Jagannath temple complex in Puri on the east coast of India is one of the sacred pilgrimage sites that adds to the attraction of its picturesque, sandy beach off the Bay of Bengal. The Ratha Yatra, the grand festival of Lord Jagannath, is celebrated every year at Puri, drawing devotees in large numbers from all over the country. They participate in a seven-day procession of the chariots of the presiding deities.

Top: The Rath Yatra at Puri.

Left: The representation of the Rath Yatra in sand on a Puri beach.

Cities
of India 🦢

HISTORIC DELHI

The capital of India is one of the oldest cities in the world, inhabited continuously for over 2,500 years. Its strategic location as the gateway to India has made it the seat of many empires – from the legendary city of Indraprastha mentioned in the Mahabharata to New Delhi, the capital of the British Empire founded in the 1920s.

Legend has it that any ruler who founded a city in Delhi would eventually be overthrown. Proving this, Delhi's landscape includes the sites of seven historic cities built by a succession of rulers over a period of 1,000 years. Like Rome, Delhi is a living museum that includes 173 national monuments and three World Heritage Sites spread across the twin cities of Old and New Delhi.

Clockwise from left: Baoli (stepwell) at Feroz Shah Kotla; The Iron Pillar at Qutub Minar; Safdarjung's Tomb; The Rashtrapati Bhavan (President's House).

MULTIFACETED MUMBAI

Bom Bahia, Bombay, Mumbai...this city on the edge of the Arabian Sea has been known by many names. Discovered by the Portuguese in 1534, this collection of seven islands was developed by the British in the 19th century into a single island that grew into a major port and trading centre. As a hub of finance and industry, Mumbai attracts Indians from all walks of life. Bollywood, the world's largest film industry, is based here. Film stars, businessmen, professionals, traders and labourers – the city accommodates them all in luxurious skyscrapers, sprawling housing estates and the world's largest slum. This gives Mumbai its cosmopolitan character and frenetic pace that's spurred by a desire to succeed or survive in this mega city.

Clockwise from facing page, top left: Chhatrapati Shivaji Terminus, formerly Victoria Terminus, better known as CST or Bombay VT; The idol of Lord Ganesh being immersed in the ocean on the last day of the Ganesh Chaturthi festival; Cinestar Shahrukh Khan in a still from the popular Bollywood film *Om Shanti Om*; Evening view of the Gateway of India, with the Taj Hotel in the background; Flora fountain in South Mumbai; A practice session of cricket at Wankhede Stadium.

THE CHARMS OF KOLKATA

Kolkata is a city of incredible contrasts: its impressive colonial monuments and decaying mansions evoke visions of colonial splendour, alongside the stark poverty of its slums. Political activism, street demonstrations and intellectual debate are an essential part of Bengali culture, giving this city a passion that few others can claim. Yet, despite its pollution and urban chaos, Kolkata's charm lies in its vibrant cultural life, its gourmet cuisine and above all, the hospitality of its people.

Clockwise from Facing Page, Top Left: The Howrah Bridge; Communism and Durga, iconic of Kolkata, are showcased in posters sold on streets; The yellow Ambassador taxi is a popular mode of transport; The Victoria Memorial; A typical colonial-era Kolkata house; A Durga Puja idol.

CHENNAI: GATEWAY TO THE SOUTH

Situated by the Bay of Bengal, the capital of Tamil Nadu has its roots in antiquity. Since the 4th century AD, this region, under powerful Pallavas and Chola kings, was famous for its seaport and magnificent temples that still remain the icons of the South Indian art and architecture. When the British arrived in the 17th century, they built Fort St George, a trading settlement that expanded into the modern city of Madras. British influence lingers in the city's tree-lined boulevards, Indo-Sarcenic buildings and the esplanade along the Marina Beach. Over the years, Chennai has successfully combined tradition with modernity. While progressing as South India's industrial hub, it has also preserved its rich cultural heritage. Its people, who are crazy about films and film stars, follow a largely traditional lifestyle. It's perhaps the best place to discover South India… from its temples and religion to its culture and cuisine.

Clockwise from Top Left: The Marina Beach; The Chennai skyline; Chennai Central Railway Station.

Clockwise from Top Left: HITECH City, a major technology township at the centre of the information technology industry in Hyderabad; Icon of Hyderabad, the historic Charminar; A flower show at the Lalbagh Botanical Garden in Bangalore, the Garden City.

THE CYBER CITIES OF HYDERABAD AND BANGALORE

Hyderabad, the capital of Andhra Pradesh, and Bangalore in Karnataka are South India's newest business destinations. Both cities have witnessed phenomenal growth as hubs of information technology and biotech research. Bangalore's Silicon Valley and Hyderabad's HITECH City now outsource their expertise to the world. Before developing into cyber cities, Hyderabad and Bangalore were heirs to a courtly culture. Bangalore was a city of stately palaces and temples, built by the kings of Mysore, before it became a British cantonment town, known for its air-conditioned climate and beautiful gardens. Hyderabad, ruled by Nizams, was one of the richest princely states of India, famed for its diamond mines and jewellery, as well as its Muslim culture and superb cuisine. The sightseeing attractions, luxury hotels and restaurants in both cities have made them popular conference destinations.

A Haven in the Hills

The hill stations of India were developed by the British in the early 19th century as summer havens to escape the heat of the plains. The British established picturesque resorts in the foothills of the Himalayas and hill ranges around the subcontinent – Shimla, Mussoorie, Dalhousie, Manali and Nainital in the north; Darjeeling and Shillong in the east; Panchgani, Mount Abu and Pachmarhi in central and west India; and Ootacamund and Coorg in the south. Here they built sanatoriums, residential schools and summer homes. At the turn of the century, better access by road and rail encouraged the annual migration to the hills, with Shimla becoming the summer capital of the Raj. Many hill stations still retain their old world charm, and new Himalayan destinations like Sikkim and Ladakh offer a wider choice of holiday havens.

SHIMLA Set around seven hills at a height of 2,000 m in the Himalayan foothills, it is North India's most popular resort. Despite the inroads of tourism, Shimla has preserved its colonial heritage as the former summer capital of the British Raj. Here you can still enjoy quiet strolls in the countryside, discover stately English landmarks and savour afternoon tea in the old-fashioned setting of a colonial hotel or club.

COOL HIMALAYAN RESORTS

Vistas of snow-clad Himalayan ranges, forests of oak, deodar and pine, meadows filled with Alpine flowers, mountain streams and shimmering lakes are some of the scenic splendours of the hill resorts of North India.

Top: Travelling on the toy train from Kalka to Shimla is quite an experience. The 96-km long journey on a historic narrow gauge railway takes six hours and offers breathtaking views of wooded valleys as it passes through 106 tunnels and 369 bridges.

NAINITAL It is the main lake resort in India's Lake District, located in the Kumaon Hills. This region, dotted with charming lake resorts, was the home of Jim Corbett, a legendary hunter and conservationist who founded the Corbett National Park nearby, one of the largest reserves for tigers.

MUSSOORIE Situated at a height of 2,000 m, 34 km from Dehradun, Mussoorie a popular tourist spot in the state of Uttarakhand. Known as the "Queen of the Hills", it offers spectacular views of the Doon Valley and the Shivalik hill ranges.

KASHMIR

The Mughals called Kashmir a paradise on earth and justified it by creating the famous Shalimar and Nishat Gardens. Today, tourists enjoy Kashmir's scenic beauty from floating houseboats on the Dal Lake in the valley of Srinagar. Two major Himalayan ranges, the Great Himalayan Range and the Pir Panjal, surround the valley from the north and south respectively. They are the source of rivers which flow down into the valleys.

Nature lovers are enchanted by Gulmarg – the Meadow of Flowers – that comes alive in spring. It was a favourite haunt of Jehangir, the Mughal king, who is said to have once collected 21 different varieties of flowers from here. Gulmarg also has the highest green golf course in the world, at an altitude of 2,650 m.

Top: A shikara drifting down the Dal lake.

Left: Pahalgam, at a height of 2,130 m, is Kashmir's premier resort.

LADAKH, a former Himalayan kingdom situated in northeast Kashmir on the border of Tibet, is one of the most remote regions of India. This Shangri-La fringed by the Karakoram and the Himalayan mountain ranges is a mystic land of snowcapped peaks and azure lakes that still preserves a flourishing Buddhist culture. Ladakh's rugged landscape offers great opportunities for mountaineering, trekking and river rafting on the Zanskar, a tributary of the Indus that flows through this region. It is said that Buddhism reached Tibet from India via Ladakh.

Ladakh's Gompas – or monasteries – are still strongholds of Tibetan Buddhism and culture. Here you can witness age-old religious traditions and see priceless treasures of Buddhist art. Many monasteries host festivals featuring plays and masked dances.

DARJEELING in West Bengal, situated at 2,100 m, offers panoramic vistas of Mount Everest and the snow-clad Kanchenjunga range from the Tiger Hill. A cable car ride on the Rangeet Valley ropeway combines unforgettable views of the Kanchenjunga range, the Sikkim valley and the Ranjeet river.

SIKKIM, situated between Nepal and Bhutan, resembles the Garden of Eden. Its wooded hills, valleys, fruit orchards and meadows – spread with orchids, rhododendrons and magnolia trees – conjure visions of a botanical paradise.

SHILLONG Discover Scotland in Shillong, located in the northeastern state of Meghalaya, at an altitude of 1,500 m above sea level. The town's lake is surrounded by mist-clad hills covered with towering pines and cascading waterfalls.

HILLS OF
THE SOUTH

COORG Also called Madikeri, Coorg is known for its coffee and spice plantations. It is home to the Coorgs, a martial race of people believed to be descended from the Arabs or Greeks.

THE NILGIRIS The scenic beauty of the Nilgiris (Blue Mountain) in South India can be experienced by travelling on the Blue Mountain Train. The route through verdant hills and tea estates passes through the hill stations of Conoor, Wellington and Lovedale before arriving at Ooty, also known as Udhagamandalam. Sample Niligiri Tea at a local tea estate and meet the Todas, tribal herdsmen who were the original inhabitants of this region.

The Call of the Wild

An amazing diversity of wildlife is sheltered in the 88 national parks and 490 wildlife sanctuaries across India – spread from Ladakh in the Himalayas to Tamil Nadu in the south. This is the country that inspired Rudyard Kipling's *Jungle Book* and Jim Corbett's *Man Eaters of Kumaon*. Its rich natural heritage includes over 350 mammal species, such as the one-horned rhino, the Himalayan ibex and the double-humped Bactrian camel. Some are endangered, like the snow leopard, the red panda, the Himalayan goat and the Nilgiri Tahir. Others are oddities, like the elephants of the Andamans that can swim up to 3 km between islands, or the robber crab that steals coconuts from palms and opens them with its claws. Shrinking natural habitats and poaching still pose a major threat to Indian wildlife, specially tigers whose numbers are dwindling despite Project Tiger, a government initiative started in 1973 to save India's national animal.

HIGHLAND RESERVES

THE HIMALAYAN NATIONAL PARK, HIMACHAL PRADESH

The Himalayas offer unspoilt reserves where one can watch wildlife in its spectacular natural surroundings. The Great Himalayan National Park near Kullu in Himachal Pradesh is a habitat for wild mountain goats, the brown bear and leopards, including the elusive snow leopard. Coniferous forests, meadows of alpine flowers, mountain streams and snowcapped peaks are part of the scenic attractions of this mountain paradise. Its rich avian population includes colourful pheasants and other Himalayan birds.

LADAKH

The uplands of Ladakh are home to many rare animals, including wild species of Tibetan horses, ass, sheep, yaks, as well as endangered species like snow leopards, ibex and the Tibetan antelope. Double-humped Bactrian camels are found in the high altitude desert regions, while the lakes around the Rupshu region are visited by flocks of migratory birds, including bar-headed geese.

TIGER TRAILS

Tigers are elusive by nature and the chances of seeing one, even in designated tiger reserves, is a matter of luck. However, if you want the thrill of tracking a tiger on an elephant's back, head for Corbett National Park in the Himalayan foothills in Uttaranchal Pradesh. The reserve is India's largest, sheltering tigers, elephants, wild boar and many species of monkeys and deer.

KANHA AND BANDHAVGARH NATIONAL PARKS in the state of Madhya Pradesh are also well known tiger reserves. Kanha was a hunting ground for English trophy hunters till the 1950s, when it was possible to bag 50 tigers in a single day's shoot here. Besides tigers, you can spot wild buffaloes and many species of deer, including the rare 12-horned variety. Bandhavgarh's hilly terrain has the highest density of tigers and chances of spotting one are guaranteed. India has 27 tiger reserves to conserve the dwindling population of tigers in the country.

OF BIRDS
AND BEASTS

KEOLADEO GHANA NATIONAL PARK, RAJASTHAN

Formerly known as the Bharatpur Bird Sanctuary, Keoladeo is a birdwatcher's paradise, where more than 300 species of birds can be seen. The lake and the wetland was artificially created by the Maharaja of Bharatpur in the 19th century. Among the many species of water birds protected here are Saras cranes, painted storks, pink flamingoes, white ibis and grey pelicans. There are also 30 birds of prey including vultures, osprey and peregrine falcons, and migratory birds which come from as far as Siberia and central Asia to spend the winters here.

GIR NATIONAL PARK, GUJARAT

The Girl National Park in Gujarat is the last refuge of the Asiatic lion, which is virtually extinct in India. Smaller and paler than the African species, some 300 Asiatic lions survive in this 260-km sanctuary.

Centuries ago, these lions were widespread in the Indo-Gangetic plains and were protected by the Mauryan Emperor Ashoka, who made the lion a symbol of his royal authority.

KAZIRANGA NATIONAL PARK, ASSAM

Set in a scenic valley surrounded by hills on the banks of the Brahmaputra river is the Kaziranga National Park, near Guwahati in the northeastern state of Assam. This is the home of the largest number of rhinos in the subcontinent, including the world's only one-horned rhino. An alarming reduction in the numbers of rhinos led to the conservation of this area in 1926, which was declared a national park in 1940. Beside rhinos, one can sight herds of wild buffalo, deer and the occasional leopard. Birdwatchers will delight in the Park's birdlife – egrets, herons, storks, fish-eating eagles and pelicans.

Facing page, from top left: A pair of Great Hornbills; the Oriental White-Eye in the Kaziranga National Park; the mighty Rhino at home in the park.

ELEPHANT COUNTRY

PERIYAR South India's most popular wildlife sanctuary, Periyar is located amid spice plantations in Kerala. Situated in the middle of this reserve is an artificial lake harbouring many birds. The surrounding forest is the home of wild elephants, bison, antelope, deer as well as tigers. The Park's scenic surroundings, nature trails and lake tours make this a fulfilling wildlife experience.

Festivals ❧ and Fairs

In India celebrations never cease as festivals happen round the year. The major festivals like Diwali, Eid or Buddha Jayanti commemorate religious events or anniversaries. Some are dedicated to a particular deity, such as Ganesh Chaturthi and Durga Puja. Others are seasonal celebrations to welcome the New Year, the advent of spring or the harvest. The most charming are cultural festivals like Rakhi, when brothers are honoured by their sisters, or Jamai Shoshti in Bengal, when sons-in-law are the guests of honour at a special feast. National days, cultural events and village fairs also add to the spirit of celebration. Whatever their origin, all festivals are marked by colourful customs and processions, and, of course, a feast, where all are welcomed with traditional hospitality.

DIWALI or Deepawali, the festival of lights in the month of October or November, is the most important event in the Hindu calendar. Homes are decorated with garlands, floor designs and lit with thousands of oil lamps to commemorate the return of Lord Ram to his kingdom in Ayodhya after 14 years of exile. Diwali marks the Hindu New Year with prayers to Lakshmi, the Goddess of Wealth. The all-night celebrations include fireworks, feasting and card games for good luck.

HOLI ushers spring with exuberance. People smear each other with colour (left) and effigies of the demon Holika are burnt to symbolise the victory of good over evil. The festival is associated with God Krishna and is celebrated with great gusto in Mathura, his birthplace.

EID is a major Muslim festival held twice a year. Eid-ul-Zuha (December) remembers Ibrahim's sacrifice with a ritual sacrifice of animals. Eid-ul-Fitr (October) is held to celebrate the end of fasting after Ramadan. Prayers are held in mosques and feasts are hosted for family and friends.

Below: Eid market stalls at the Jama Masjid in New Delhi. *Right:* Children celebrate *Eid-ul-Fitr* at the Jama Masjid.

DUSSHERA is a 10-day festival in the month of September or October, symbolising the victory of good over evil. In North India, towering effigies of the demon Ravana are burnt to symbolise the destruction of evil.

DURGA PUJA In West Bengal, manifestations of the Goddess Durga slaying the buffalo demon Mahishasura are worshipped during the festival of Durga Puja.

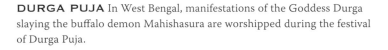

GANESH CHATURTHI Over 10 days in September, images of Ganesh are worshipped in homes and street corners in Maharashtra, climaxing with the immersion of these idols in the sea on the 11th day, accompanied by scenes of religious fervour.

Clockwise from Top Left: Effigy of the demon-king Ravana put up for burning; A Durga Puja procession; A devotee carries the idol of Ganesh for immersion in the sea.

JANMASTAMI

The birthday of Lord Krishna, the most popular among the Hindu gods, is celebrated in the month of August. Legends of Krishna stealing butter from a hanging pot are enacted by devotees during this festival. Dance dramas on Krishna's life are also staged, especially in his birthplace Mathura.

GOA CARNIVAL

Introduced by the Portuguese in Goa, this three-day carnival, held before Lent, is a time of merry making with music, dancing and costume parades, presided by Momo, the King of the Carnival.

SOUTHERN CELEBRATIONS

THRISSUR POORAM In South India's most spectacular temple pageant in April or May, presiding deities from temples around Kerala are brought to Thrissur temple in a cavalcade of elephants, accompanied by attending priests and musicians. The highlight is the competition between two rival temples, featuring displays of colourful parasols, musical concerts and fireworks.

PONGAL The harvest festival of Tamil Nadu is celebrated in January, when offerings of rice and sugarcane are made to Surya, the sun god. Homes are spring cleaned and decorated with *kolams* (designs made with rice flour). The act of boiling over of milk in the clay pot is considered auspicious, indicating future prosperity for the family.

ONAM The harvest festival of Kerala is celebrated around September for 10 days. It also marks the return of Mahabali, a legendary demon king, to his kingdom here. Festivities include feasts, cultural shows, temple processions and a fiercely competitive boat race – the Snake Boat Race held on the Pampa river – among rowing teams from neighbouring villages.

Top: The Snake Boat Race marking the festival of Onam in Kerala.

Left: The elephant procession at the Thrissur Pooram festival in Kerala.

FAIRS AND FIESTAS

PUSHKAR FAIR

The village of Pushkar in Rajasthan comes alive for an annual cattle fair (October or November) attended by villagers in colourful traditional costumes. Pushkar is also a place of pilgrimage for devotees who come to worship at the Brahma temple here and bathe in its holy lake.

DESERT FESTIVAL, JODHPUR

Jodhpur's Desert Festival – in the month of January or February – offers an opportunity to witness the colourful culture of Rajasthan through performances of folk music and dance that are particular to a community of nomadic clan.

SURAJ KUND CRAFTS MELA

It is the country's biggest crafts fair held in the outskirts of Delhi in February. Here you can pick up handlooms, handicrafts and furniture, directly from weavers and craftsmen who come from all over India.

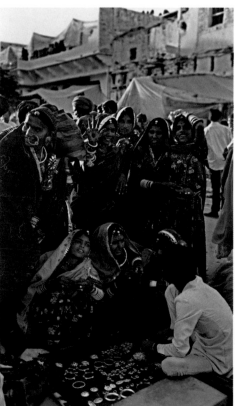

KHAJURAHO DANCE FESTIVAL

Witness classical dance performances by famous Indian artistes against the dramatic backdrop of the famous temples of Khajuraho at this annual festival held in February or March.

VILLAGE FAIRS

Popular means of entertainment and trade, village fairs are packed with colourful extravaganza. Some interesting features include folk music and dance, cattle market and puppet show.

The Culinary Melting Pot

An Indian meal can be a voyage of discovery into one of the most sophisticated cuisines in the world that evolved from ayurvedic traditions in 3000 BC. Ayurveda promoted a balanced diet, flavoured by medicinal herbs and spices, that became the foundation of India's curry cuisine. Hindu taboos on eating beef developed into a tradition of vegetarianism that was reinforced by Buddhism and Jainism in the 6th century BC.

India's culinary heritage encompasses the widest choice of regional cuisines, influenced by the country's geography, climate, religion and culture. These cuisines acquired their distinctive flavour from local foods and spices and often included specialities developed by different communities. They were further enhanced by new ingredients and cooking styles introduced by the Mughals, Portuguese, British and Arabs, resulting in a rich culinary culture.

VEGETARIAN A typical vegetarian meal includes lentils, vegetables, yoghurt, rice and Indian breads, accompanied by pickles, condiments and a dessert. Traditionally all the courses are presented together on a *thali* or platter.

RICH REGIONAL FLAVOURS

Diversity is the keynote of regional cuisines that have been shaped by religious beliefs as well as local cultures. A large percentage of Indians are vegetarian and their cuisine is unparalleled in its variety and range of flavours. Mughlai cuisine was adapted with variations in royal courts across India, giving rise to distinctive culinary traditions. The Portuguese and British left their impact on the cuisine of Christian communities, especially in Goa and Kolkata, while the Arabs enhanced the Muslim specialities of Kerala. Zoroastrians and Jews infused their culinary culture with Indian ingredients and spices to create dishes that were unique to their community.

WAZWAN is one of the specialities of Kashmir's cuisine, influenced by the Mughals in their use of fruits, nuts and aromatic spices. This 32-course banquet prepared by special chefs features an extravagant array of meat and vegetable dishes, ending with Kahwa – flavoured green tea.

SOUTH INDIAN CUISINE

The South Indian food is mainly rice-based. Rice is combined with lentils in the preparation of idlis, dosas, uttapams and vadas. Most of the vegetarian and non-vegetarian dishes of the south have a generous use of spices and coconuts, found in abundance in this region. The final tempering with oil, mustard seeds, curry leaves, red chillies and urad dhal is typical to South India. While Andhra Pradesh is famous for its biryani and kebabs, the staple food of Kerala is fish with rice.

COURTLY CUISINES

Creating a feast for kings was the inspiration for classic cuisines that developed in Delhi, Lucknow and Hyderabad – cities that are famed for their food even today.

MUGHLAI CUISINE

The Mughals brought the sophistication of the Persian court with its tradition of fine dining. They also introduced baked breads and barbecued meats cooked in a tandoor or clay oven. Royal cooks innovated with central Asian dishes to create aromatic pilaus, kebabs and rich curries cooked with almonds, raisins and cream to create the famous Mughlai cuisine. The gastronomic legacy of the Mughals remains an integral part of the Indian table for weddings and celebrations.

AVADHI CUISINE

Cuisine was perfected into an art form by the Nawabs of Lucknow, who were great gourmets. Chefs were paid extravagant amounts to create innovative specialities such as pilaus coloured to resemble gems. Lucknow is famous for its kebabs and biryanis that are still prepared according to royal recipes. Though influenced by Mughal cuisine, Avadhi cuisine is distinguished by its subtle spicing and lighter flavours, imparted by a process of slow, steam cooking known as Dum Pukht.

From Left to Right: A Mughlai platter; Spices of India; Avadhi cuisine.

OUR FAST FOOD NATION

Eating out can be a literal experience in India, where every city has pavement stalls offering a round-the-clock menu of quick meals and snacks. Some of the best food can be sampled in roadside restaurants called *dhabas*. Started by Punjabi immigrants who came to Delhi after India's partition, they offered barbecued meats and *naans* (leavened breads), popular in Pakistan. It is said that famous Punjabi dishes like Chicken Tikka and Butter Chicken were innovated here. So whether you stop for a snack or a mini-meal, these roadside eateries offer a taste of India in bite-size morsels.

POPULAR STREET FOOD

Kathi (skewer) kebabs mixed with onions and spices and wrapped in unleavened Indian breads is a popular Indian takeaway.

South Indian breakfast foods such as dosa and idlis have crossed geographic borders and are now served at every street corner.

Left: All the world stops for chaat – fried, wheat flour discs served with dumplings, topped with spiced yoghurt and a variety of tangy sauces.

For the Indian craftsman, the act of creation was an offering to the gods. This demanded a high degree of perfection that evolved over the ages by adorning temples, monuments and palaces. Since the 2nd century BC, visitors to India, like the Greek traveller Megasthenes and the Chinese pilgrim Huien Tsang, have marvelled at the craftsmanship of Indian artisans. Royal patronage

Arts and Crafts

helped arts and crafts to flourish and provided the impetus for innovation and creativity. Objects of daily use were fashioned into works of art that combined beauty with utility. Classic traditions and skills, along with a vibrant legacy of folk art and crafts, were preserved intact by generations of artists, craftsmen and weavers in towns and villages. All this has contributed to a dazzling heritage in art, textiles and handicraft, making India a shopper's paradise.

WONDROUS WEAVES AND EMBROIDERY

For centuries, India has been famed for its muslins, brocades and patterned silks that have been exported to the world. Today this rich textile tradition is enhanced by constant innovation, thus keeping pace with contemporary trends while preserving classic styles.

SARIS

Every bride's trousseau in India includes saris from Varanasi and Kanjeevaram. Varanasi (also known as Benares) produces brocades and tissue saris with delicate patterns and motifs in gold and silver thread. Kanjeevaram in Tamil Nadu is famed for its silk fabrics and saris that are woven in exotic shades. The saris are embellished with gold or silk thread motifs and have vivid contrasting borders.

DHURRIES AND CARPETS

There is a wide choice in floor coverings – from cotton dhurries to silk and woollen carpets and woven reed mats. Dhurries in colourful woven designs are produced all over India, especially in Punjab, Rajasthan and Karnataka. Woollen and silk carpets feature Persian designs and motifs introduced by the Mughals. Woven reed and palm mats are used in village homes all over India – the most interesting are from Assam, Tripura and Kerala.

EMBROIDERY

Every region has ethnic styles of embroidery that embellish traditional costumes, bedspreads and wall hangings. Mughal Zardozi work with gold and silver wire is in vogue for wedding outfits and high fashion garments. Punjab's Phulkari designs on shawls and bedcovers were originally made for the bride's trousseau. Lucknow's Chikan work has delicate designs on muslin that are as popular today as they were in the Mughal era. Kantha embroidery of Bihar and Bengal comprises floral, animal and bird motifs on both cotton and silk. Kashmiri embroidery ranges from hand embroidery on shawls to machine stitched, crewel work on rugs and furnishings. Village women in Gujarat, Rajasthan and Karnataka are known for their colourful embroidered costumes decorated with beads, mirrors and appliqués.

Facing page: Traditional carpet weaving at a village near Luni, Rajasthan.

Clockwise from Top Left: Patola from Gujarat; Baluchari from Bengal; Kutch embroidery.

PAINTINGS AND CARVINGS

Rooted in tradition, Indian art covers many styles from classic Mughal and Rajput miniature paintings and murals to folk and tribal art, executed on paper, canvas, cloth, bark wood and ivory. The best-known examples include Ajanta murals in Aurangabad, Tanjore paintings from Tamil Nadu, Madhubani paintings from Bihar, Kamalkari paintings from Andhra Pradesh and Pithoro paintings from Gujarat.

TANJORE PAINTINGS hail from the temple town of Thanjavur, near Chennai. These religious icons are adorned with gold and embedded with semi-precious stones that give it a multi-dimensional effect.

The skills of Indian craftsmen are displayed in decorative carvings in stone, marble and wood. These are available in a choice of items from statues, carved windows and doors to decorative artefacts for the home.

Jammu and Kashmir, Uttar Pradesh, Gujarat, Karnataka and Kerala have distinctive styles of wood carvings. In Uttar Pradesh, Saharanpur is known for its vine-Ieaf patterns in hard sheesham and Mainpuri is famous for its wood-work inlaid with brass wire on ebony or black sheesham. Rajasthan is noted for its carved sandalwood and rosewood furniture.

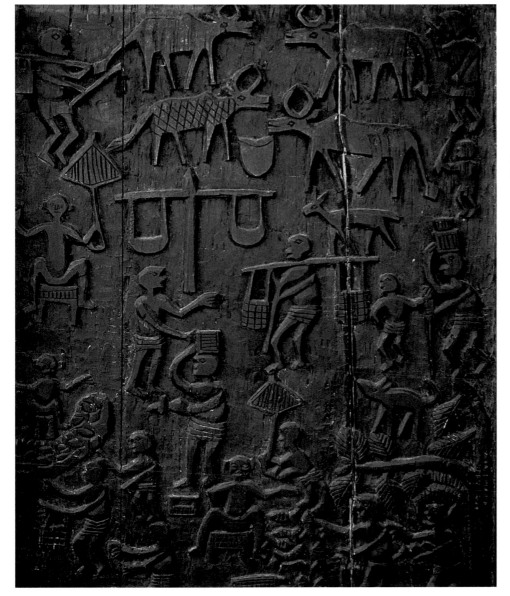

Clockwise from Left: Wooden carving on a door in Raighar museum, Chhattisgarh; Gods and goddesses carved on wood; Inlay work on Salim Chishti's Tomb in Agra.

PIETRA DURA This Italian art of setting stone within a stone was introduced in India by the Mughals to decorate their monuments. The Taj Mahal is the most exquisite example of this art form, where as many as 35 different semi-precious stones have been used in a single floral motif.

METAL WORK

India was one of the earliest countries in the world to discover metallurgy. Since 3000 BC, metal workers have been producing fine sculptures, artefacts and utensils in bronze, brass, copper and iron, decorated in specialised styles.

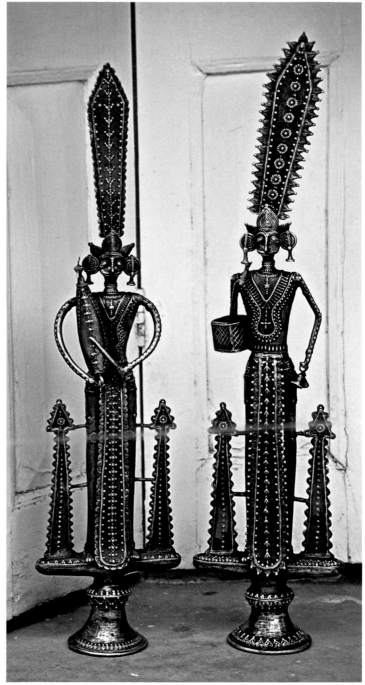

Clockwise from Top Left: A workshop of metal work; Bell metal work of Bastar, Chhattisgarh; A bronze sculpture; A brass sculpture; A Rajasthani artefact.

A variety of metal work styles are seen in different parts of India. Benares produces moulded and incised brassware as bowls, flasks, plates and trays. Karnataka specialises in inlaid design on silver on an alloy of copper and zinc known as Bidri. Copper items are incised with floral designs in Kashmir and studded with brass decoration in Ladakh. Bastar in Bihar is known for its Dhokra or bell metal figurines and bowls made by the lost wax process.

JEWELLERY

Every state in India has a unique style of traditional jewellery, such as the temple jewellery from Nagercoil and fine filigree work in silver from Orissa and Andhra Pradesh.

MEENAKARI AND KUNDAN Jaipur is famous for enamelled jewellery known as Meenakari, where enamelled designs on gold and silver are used to adorn jewellery. Delhi is known for kundan or the setting of semi-precious or precious stones in gold jewellery. These uncut gems are backed with silver foil to make the stones sparkle and shine.

SACRED JEWELS

The Navaratna pendant and the Rudraksha necklace have a significance in the Hindu mythology, where they are used to invoke the nine *grahas* (planets) and Lord Shiva.

SILVER The village brides are adorned in silver ornaments from head to toe. These ornaments are a symbol of a bride's wealth that can be sold for cash in times of need.

The Adventure ❧ Trail

For discerning travellers, India is emerging as an exciting destination for adventure sports. The country's geographic diversity – snow clad mountain ranges, alpine valleys, mountain streams and mighty rivers, tropical forests and beaches – provide opportunities to enjoy a wide range of sports. Mountaineering and trekking in the Himalayas; parasailing and paragliding across scenic plains; river rafting in the Indus, Beas and Ganga rivers; fishing in mountain streams and rivers; camel safaris across the Thar Desert; or scuba diving in the Andaman and Nicobar Islands – there is something for everyone. India is an international venue for golf and polo, while cycling and motorcycle tours are becoming popular among biking enthusiasts.

RIVER RAFTING Nothing can match the adrenaline high of river rafting in the waters of the Upper Ganga from Rishikesh to Devprayag, rated as one of the most exciting runs for this sport. Rivers in Ladakh, Sikkim and tributaries of the Ganga also offer excellent options for amateur as well as expert rafters.

CAMEL SAFARIS A camel safari across the Thar Desert in western Rajasthan is the best way to discover the vibrant life and culture of the desert. Safaris ranging from one to four days come equipped with guides, cooks and mobile tents for camping on the dunes.

POLO Jodhpur in Rajasthan is the home of Polo, where Jodhpur riding breeches were invented. Babur, the founder of the Mughal dynasty, is credited with making the sport popular in the 15th century. Polo matches are held in Delhi, Kolkata, Jaipur, Jodhpur and Mumbai.

OTHER ADVENTURE SPORTS

PARAGLIDING Billing, located at 2,600 m in the Kangra Valley in Himachal Pradesh, offers the ideal climate and topography for all levels of paragliders. Besides Himachal Pradesh, there are great paragliding sites in Uttaranchal, Rajasthan and Maharashtra. The best locales for parasailing are in the hill resorts of Manali, Darjeeling, the Nilgiris in South India and Gangtok in Sikkim.

MOUNTAINEERING For serious mountaineers, the Himalayas offer the thrill of scaling some of the world's highest peaks, reaching up to 7,000 m. The most challenging peaks are located in Sikkim, Ladakh, Uttaranchal and Himachal Pradesh.

TREKKING A trekking holiday in India can be as tough or easy as you want it to be – excursions to high altitude mountains and alpine meadows or easy walks through scenic hills and orchards. The major trekking areas in the western Himalayas cover the states of Jammu and Kashmir, Uttaranchal and Himachal Pradesh. In the eastern Himalayas, the trekking trail extends from Darjeeling in West Bengal to the states of Sikkim and Arunachal Pradesh in the northeast.

ANGLING Rivers, mountain streams and lakes offer a wide choice for angling holidays in India. Among the many species of freshwater fish is the prized Mahaseer. Kashmir is a paradise for trout, while the coasts of Goa and Kerala offer deep sea fishing in motor boats.

SKIING India has some excellent locales for skiing. Some of the best ski destinations are in the Kumaon hills, Jammu and Kashmir, Himachal Pradesh and the northeastern parts of India. Aquatic activities like deep sea diving, scuba diving, snorkeling and underwater photography can be enjoyed in the islands of Andaman and Nicobar and Lakshadweep.

Clockwise from Facing Page: Trekkers crossing the river over a log bridge in Uttarakhand; Skiing in Gulmarg, Jammu and Kashmir; Parasailing in the mountains.

Land of
~ Spirituality

Religion is an intrinsic part of the Indian life, finding expression in the country's monuments and lending colour to its art, traditions and festivals. A quest for spirituality has resulted in the evolution of four major religions here – Hinduism, Buddhism, Jainism and Sikhism. Its people have also embraced Islam and Christianity, while offering religious freedom to communities of Jews and Zoroastrians who settled here.

Hinduism, the predominant religion, is practised by 82 percent of India's population. Hindu traditions, dating back to antiquity, include many forms of devotion, from nature worship to veneration of a pantheon of gods and goddesses, dominated by three main deities – Brahma, the Creator; Vishnu, the Preserver; and Shiva, the Destroyer of the Universe. Within this framework are a multitude of sects, founded by popular saints or teachers. This multiplicity of beliefs has given Hinduism a spirit of tolerance, allowing many faiths to flourish.

Buddhism and Jainism developed around the 6th century BC as a reaction against orthodox Hinduism. Both religions evolved paths to salvation based on a code of ethics, non-violence and compassion towards all living beings. Muslim invaders brought Islam to India in the 16th century BC. Its philosophy of equality found favour in a society riddled by caste divisions. Today Muslims account for 12 percent of the population. Christianity's roots in India date back to the arrival of St Thomas the Apostle in South India in 52 AD. Missionaries who came with European colonisers in the 16th century were responsible for the spread of Christianity in India. Sikhism, founded in the 15th century by Guru Nanak, is a comparatively new religion. The Sikhs believe in one God, revealed in the teachings of their 10 Gurus, contained in their holy book, the Guru Granth Sahib.

KUMBH MELA

According to legend, Allahabad is one of the places (along with Haridwar, Nasik and Ujjain) where drops from a sacred pot of nectar fell during a battle of the gods and demons. This event is celebrated during the Kumbh Mela, a religious festival held in rotation at these places, once in 12 years. The Maha Kumbh Mela is the most auspicious, when thousands of pilgrims and holy men from all over India get together at Allahabad to bathe in the river during a special planetary conjunction.

Clockwise from Top Left: A holy man at the Ardh Kumb Mela at Allahabad; People taking a holy dip in the Ganga in Haridwar during the Kumbh Mela; A priest performing a puja on the banks of the Ganga in Haridwar.

HARIDWAR AND RISHIKESH: THE GATEWAY TO THE GODS

Haridwar and Rishikesh are ancient Hindu pilgrimage sites on the banks of the sacred river Ganga, in the Himalayan foothills. They are also the gateways to the Himalayan shrines of Kedarnath and Badrinath, dedicated to Shiva and Vishnu respectively. Pilgrims come to Haridwar and Rishikesh to pay homage to the gods and wash their sins in the waters of this holy river.

HARIDWAR

The evening aarti ceremony on the riverbank is an exalting experience, as priests light thousands of lamps and invoke the gods to the sound of cymbals and bells. Devotees offer prayers by floating hundreds of oil lamps in the river . . . a magical sight!

SHRINES AND MONASTERIES

While Buddhism and Jainism originated 2500 years ago, Sikhism is a comparatively new religion, founded in the 15th century. Nevertheless, it is more popular in India than either Buddhism or Jainism.

THE GOLDEN TEMPLE

A feeling of tranquillity pervades the Golden Temple in Amritsar, the spiritual centre of the Sikhs. This white marble complex with gilded domes, also known as Harmandir Sahib, stands in the centre of an artificial lake called the Amrit Sarovar (Pool of Nectar). It was built in the 16th century by the Sikh Guru Arjan Das, on foundations laid by a Muslim saint. The shrine was destroyed by the Afghans in 1761 and rebuilt by Maharaja Ranjit Singh who donated the gold to decorate its façade and interiors. Every Sikh aspires to visit this shrine to listen to recitations of the Guru Granth Sahib (the holy book of the Sikhs) and devotional hymns sung from dawn to dusk. In accordance with Sikh beliefs, the Golden Temple welcomes visitors of all faiths and serves free meals to 10,000 guests daily at its *langar* (communal kitchen).

BANGLA SAHIB AND NANAK PIAO

In Delhi, Bangla Sahib and Nanak Piao are two popular Sikh pilgrimage sites, built in the memory of the eighth Guru Sri Harkishan and the first Guru Nanak Dev, respectively.

Clockwise from Top: The Golden Temple; Gurudwara Bangla Sahib; Gurudwara Nanak Piao.

Clockwise from Top: The statue of Buddha in Shey Monastery; Tibetan Budhhist prayer stones in Ladakh; A monk praying in a monastery.

THE MONASTERIES OF DHARAMSALA AND LADAKH

After reaching a peak at the beginning of the first millennium AD, Buddhism suffered a decline in the country of its origin till the 1950s, when a revival of Buddhism attracted new disciples to the faith. In the meantime, the religion spread to south Asia and the Far East from India. Though many Indian cities have modern Buddhist temples, practising monasteries are located in states that have a majority of Tibetan Buddhists. The Gompas or monasteries in Dharamsala, Darjeeling, Ladakh and Sikkim, built in the Tibetan style and decorated with colourful murals, painting and sculptures, are distinctively different from the Buddhist temples in the rest of the country. Dharamsala in Himachal Pradesh is the home of the Dalai Lama and its Namgyal Monastery is a religious centre for a large population of Tibetan refugees.

FAITHS FROM OUTSIDE

India's 120 million Muslims form the world's second largest Muslim community. Here, religious minorities like the Christians, Jews and Zoroastrians practise their faith with a distinctive Indian ethos.

JAMA MASJID, DELHI Among the mosques in India, the most spectacular is the Jama Masjid, opposite the Red Fort in Delhi. Designed by Shah Jehan in 1656, this mosque was the religious focus of the city of Shahjehanabad. Built in white marble, it is decorated with strips of red sandstone and black marble that outline its graceful domes and minarets. One of the largest mosques in India, it can accommodate 25,000 devotees at a time. During the festival of Eid, the sighting of the moon is announced from this mosque.

BASILICA OF BOM JESUS

The Portuguese ruled Goa from 1510 to 1961, and many of Goa's historic churches were built during the colonial rule. Some of the most magnificent churches like the Basilica of Bom Jesus and the Se Cathedral are preserved in Old Goa, the former capital of the colony, now a World Heritage Site.

The Cathedral of Bom Jesus is dedicated to the Infant Jesus and is famous as the resting place of St Francis Xavier whose remains are enshrined here. St Francis Xavier came to India with the Portuguese to spread the message of Christianity. He died on a voyage to China in 1552. When, in accordance to his wishes, his body was transferred to Goa a year later, it was miraculously found as fresh as the day on which it was buried. The body was preserved in an air tight coffin made of glass and placed inside a silver casket, which is lowered once every decade for public viewing.

The church is built in the Renaissance style with lavishly decorated Baroque interiors, seen in its carved and gilded main altar and the mausoleum of St Francis Xavier. The three-tiered tomb constructed in white marble and jasper was designed by a Florentine sculptor, Giovanni Batista Foggini, a gift from the Duke of Tuscany. The Church is a pilgrimage spot for Christians, especially during the exposition of the sacred relics, held every ten years.

ZOROASTRIANISM AND JUDAISM

The highly educated and prosperous Parsi or Zoroastrian community, hailing from Persia (present day Iran), has found a permanent abode in India. Having enriched India educationally, industrially, economically and culturally, the community is now unfortunately disintegrating, owing to religious and social reasons. Jews arrived in India 2500 years ago and have established themselves in Kerala, Maharashtra, West Bengal, Mizoram and Manipur, with their largest concentration in Mumbai. Though a large part of the Jewish community has migrated from India, they have left behind them a rich legacy of synagogues.

Clockwise from Top Left: Basilica of Bom Jesus; A Parsi priest performing the Jashan ceremony; The interior of a Jewish synagogue in Cochin, Kerala.

Healing  Touch

The world is now discovering the benefits of ayurveda and yoga, practised in India for centuries. India's ancient healing traditions include some of the world's oldest systems of medicine – ayurveda, siddha and unani – that have influenced herbal medicine in Tibet, China, Southeast Asia and the Middle East. All three schools of medicine have specialised training institutes and hospitals that supplement healthcare facilities in India.

Besides this, the country also has a rich tradition of folk medicine that is still used in villages. These range from home remedies for common ailments to herbal treatments and drugs prescribed by *vaids* or herbal healers. Other alternative systems of medicine are naturopathy, homeopathy as well as Reiki and Pranic healing that employ psychic energy to heal the body.

THE SCIENCE OF YOGA

The principles of yoga were founded on disciplines practised by Indian ascetics. This was later written down in the Vedas and codified into a text by the sage Patanjali. Yoga is a life science that promotes a perfect balance of body, mind and spirit, through techniques of meditation, breathing and physical exercise. It aims to produce an elevated state of consciousness, leading to mental and spiritual harmony.

Yoga is the only discipline that is able to cure diseases without the use of drugs. It is widely used as a part of Ayurvedic treatments to cure asthma, diabetes and blood pressure among many other ailments. Modern medicine has recognised the benefits of yoga in preventing diseases and alleviating stress, making it popular worldwide.

Top: East meets west at Ananda, an international spa, set in Rishikesh in the Himalayas. Here, Western spa treatments are combined with Eastern healing techniques, including ayurveda and yoga, to rejuvenate both body and mind.
Right: A relaxing soak at the Mandawa resort spa.

HERBAL HEALING IN KERALA

Ayurveda, meaning the Knowledge of Life, is a holistic system of medicine that originated in India 5,000 years ago. It incorporates a body of knowledge, discovered by Indian sages that are outlined in the Vedas. Ayurveda promotes a balance of body, mind and spirit through a regimen of meditation, diet, exercise and cleansing routines. It also includes rejuvenating and therapeutic treatments designed to promote physical well being.

Kerala in South India is the home of ayurveda, influenced by the healing traditions of the Siddhi school and perfected by traditional physicians known as Astavaidayans. These physicians used medicinal herbs and plants that are endemic to this region in treating various diseases. Kerala's ayurvedic hospitals and spas now attract a global clientele.

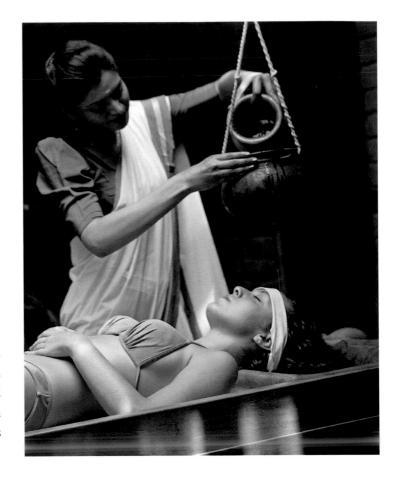

KERALA MASSAGE Kerala's spas offer special massages by trained masseurs, using medicated oils and herbs that are rubbed into the body. The oil massages are categorised into rejuvenative, preventive and curative massages. Rejuvenating therapy is the most popular, where two oils are chosen according to the constituency of one's body and massaged all over to stimulate and revitalise the body.

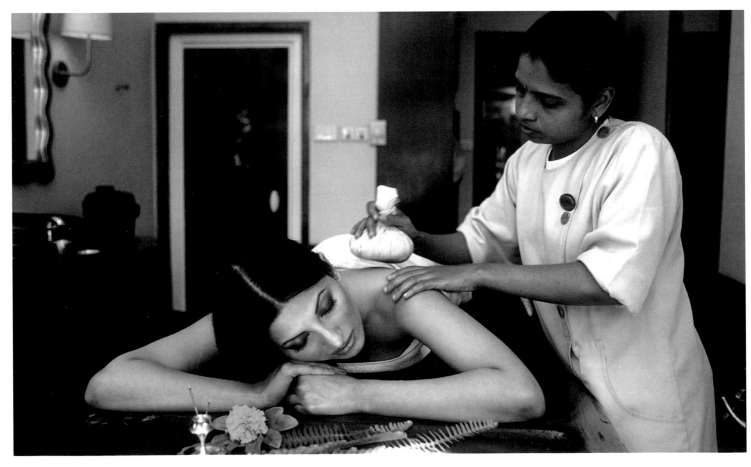

KALARIPAYATTU (above) This oldest form of martial arts, dating back to more than 2000 years, is indigenous to Kerala. This traditional psycho-physiological discipline, rooted in Kerala's unique mytho-historical heritage, is a scientific system of physical culture training.

YOGA AND MEDITATION (below) The serene environs of Kerala are the perfect ambience for rejuvenating the mind and body with yoga and meditation. The spa treatments should be supplemented with a visit to yoga centres in Kerala, which help in attaining peace and tranquillity.

PICTURE CREDITS

ARUN H.C. / IndiaPicture pp 45b

AUSTA SANJAY / IndiaPicture pp 39tr, 21b

BAKSHI AKHIL / IndiaPicture pp 39tl

BHATTACHARYA BHASWARAN / IndiaPicture pp 16t, 16b

BRANDON MATT / IndiaPicture pp 48

CAMA SHERNAZ / IndiaPicture pp 91bl

CARAVELLA, WAYNE and MIRIAM / IndiaPicture pp 62b

CHAMARIA PRADEEP / IndiaPicture pp 81t

CHATTERJEE AVIK / IndiaPicture pp 82

DAS BIKAS / IndiaPicture pp 85tl

DHINGRA N.C. pp 52, 53b, 58, 59b

DUBE D.N. / IndiaPicture pp 7br, 9br

FLORE LAMOUREUX / IndiaPicture pp 9t, 63b

GUPTA VARUN / IndiaPicture pp 85b, 86–87

HARAN K. / IndiaPicture pp 41b

INDIAPICTURE pp 60tr

JOHNSTON CLINTON / IndiaPicture pp 38t, 25b

KHAZANCHI B.N. / IndiaPicture pp 20, 26t, 12t, 30, 31bl, 19br, 67tr

KUMAR CHITRANGAD / IndiaPicture pp 61t

KUMAR I.S. / IndiaPicture pp 83t

MEHTA HEMANT / IndiaPicture pp 68b, 69b, 71b, 70b, 60b, 92l

MENON ANUSHKA / IndiaPicture pp 89t

MUTHURAMAN V. / IndiaPicture pp 18t, 18b, 64–65

NATH ASHOK / IndiaPicture pp 36t

OSAN GURINDER / IndiaPicture pp 85tr, 89bl

PASRICHA AMIT / IndiaPicture pp 36b, 49tr, 78cl, 95b

RESHII MARRYAM / IndiaPicture pp 76

ROUT BISWARANJAN / IndiaPicture pp 37t, 37b

SACHDEVA RAJEEV / IndiaPicture pp 5c, 8t, 28t, 28b, 73c, 88t

SAMARPAN AMANO pp 54t, 54b, 57t, 57b

SARAN SHALINI / IndiaPicture pp 5b, 21t, 23tl, 26b, 27b, 33b, 66tc, 67bl, 71t, 75b, 77b, 79br, 91br

SEN SUMIT pp 42–43

SHANKAR SONDEEP / SAABPIX pp 2–3, 4t, 4c, 4b, 5t, 6, 7tl, 7tr, 8br, 19bl, 23t, 23b, 25t, 32t, 32bl, 32br, 33tl, 33tr, 34, 35t, 35bl, 35br, 38–39b, 40t, 40bl, 40br, 41tl, 44t, 44bl, 44br, 45tl, 46, 47t, 47c, 47b, 50, 51t, 51b, 56t, 56b, 59t, 62tr, 65r, 66bl, 66br, 69tl, 69tr, 73tl, 73tr, 73b, 75tl, 75tr, 77tr, 78bl, 78br, 83b, 84, 88br, 89br, 90, 93t, 93bl, 93br, 94t, 94b, 95t

SHARMA ANIL KUMAR / IndiaPicture pp 12b, 14–15, 22b, 29, 62bl

SHARMA ASHOO / IndiaPicture pp 31tc, 77tl, 78tl, 78tr

SHARMA M.D. / IndiaPicture pp 22t, 31br, 67br, 81b

SHARMA PULKIT / IndiaPicture pp 17tl

SHARMA RAHUL / IndiaPicture pp 13, 27t, 74,

SHARMA SHYAM SUNDER / IndiaPicture pp 80

SHIEKH MUSHTAQ / Om Books Internatinoal pp 41tr

SINGH PUNEET / IndiaPicture pp 62tl

SINHA VIVEK pp 53t, 54–55

THAKUR RAJEEV / IndiaPicture pp 63t

USMANI SALMAN / IndiaPicture pp 72t

VASANTHI R. / IndiaPicture pp 8bl

WADHWA RAJINDER / IndiaPicture pp 72br, 88bl

WALIA B.P.S. / IndiaPicture pp 16bl, 19t, 24, 92tl